Contents

Our world would be a very different place without machines to help us.

Simple Technology
Pulleys

written by Mandy Suhr
and illustrated by Mike Gordon

First published in Great Britain in 1996
by Wayland (Publishers) Ltd
This edition printed in 2001 by Hodder Wayland

This revised edition published in 2009 by Wayland,
338 Euston Road, London NW1 3BH

Wayland Australia,
Level 17/207 Kent Street, Sydney, NSW 2000

Copyright © Wayland 1996

British Library Cataloguing in Publication Data
Suhr, Mandy.
   Pulleys. -- (Simple technology)
   1. Pulleys--Juvenile literature. 2. Power
   transmission--Juvenile literature.
   I. Title II. Series
   621.8'5-dc22

ISBN 978-0-7502-5952-1

Printed in China

Wayland is a division of Hachette Children's Books,
an Hachette UK Company, www.hachette.co.uk

A pulley is a simple lifting machine.

The idea for a pulley may have come from someone throwing a rope over a tree branch to help them to lift a heavy load.

They discovered that it was easier to lift a heavy weight by pulling downwards rather than pushing upwards.

You attach one end of the rope to the object you want to lift and pass the rope around the groove of the wheel of the pulley. When you pull the other end of the rope, you can raise the object.

PULLEY WHEEL

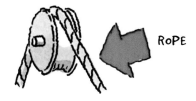 ROPE

Today's pulleys are made up of a wheel with a groove around the rim and a rope.

LOAD

EFFORT

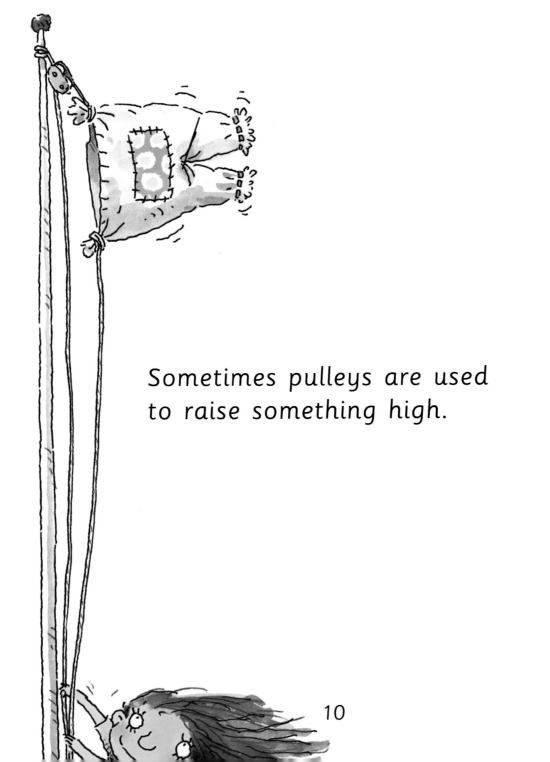

Sometimes pulleys are used
to raise something high.

It is much easier to use a pulley than to climb up a flagpole and put the flag on top.

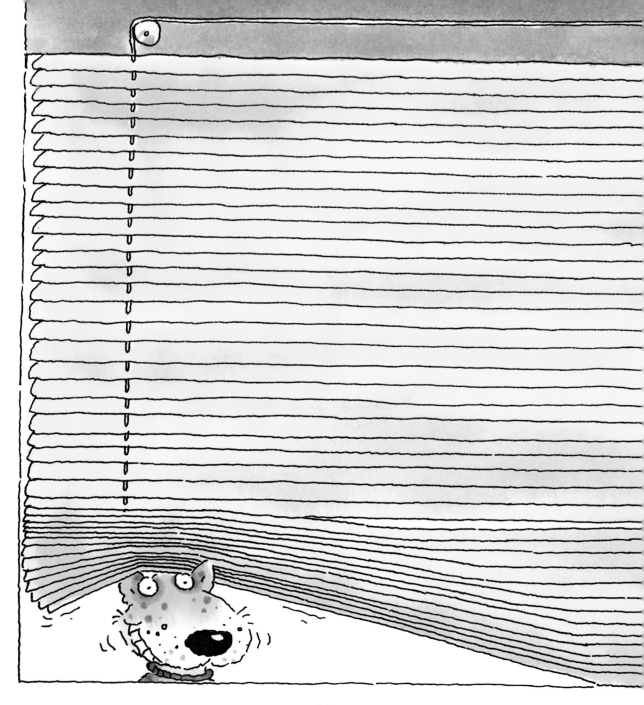

You use a pulley to raise a blind.

You may even be attached
to a pulley in hospital.

Pulleys are also used to lift heavy loads. It is easier to pull downwards to lift a heavyweight because you can use your own body weight. Your body acts as a counter-weight.

The more pulley wheels you use,
the easier the job of lifting becomes.
Using two pulley wheels you can
lift something twice as heavy as
you can with one pulley wheel.

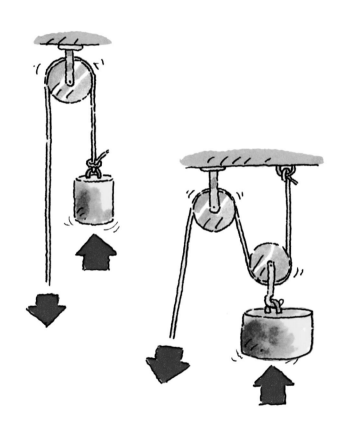

Experiment 1

Experiment 2

20

Three pulley wheels let you lift something three times as heavy.

Experiment 3

Cranes use lots of
pulley wheels all
together so they can
lift really heavy loads
from place to place.

23

When you travel in a lift, you are using a pulley. The lift car is raised by strong cables around a pulley wheel.

An electric motor drives
the pulley to raise the lift.

Make your own pulley flagpole

You will need:
- 2 plastic bottle tops
- 2 one inch nails
- 30 cm length of square wooden dowling
- a cereal box
- PVA glue
- some string
- An adult to help you

1. Ask an adult to nail one bottle top to the top of the wooden dowling and one about 20 cm farther down. They must be loose enough to turn.

2. Turn the cereal box on its side and mark around the base of the dowling. Cut out the hole and slot your flag pole in to its base. Decorate the base.

3. Cut out a paper flag
and colour it with
your own design.
Fold over one edge.

4. Lay your string along
the fold with the centre
in the middle of the flag.
Glue the edge down. Leave to dry.

5. Tie the string around the bottle tops so
that it is quite tight. Now when you
pull down on one side of the string,
you will hoist your flag!

Glossary

Cable   A very strong rope, often made of metal.

Counter -weight   A weight used to pull down the weight end of a rope when an object is being lifted at the other end.

Crane   A large machine used for lifting very heavy objects.

Load   The weight of an object that is moved by a machine.

Pulley   A wheel with a rope around it, used to lift an object up.

Rim   The outer edge of a wheel.

Notes for adults

Simple Technology is a series of elementary books designed to introduce young children to the everyday machines that make our lives easier, and the basic principles behind them.

For millions of years people have been inventing and using machines to make work easier. These machines have been constantly modified and redesigned over the years to make them more sophisticated and more successful at their task. This is really what technology is all about. It is the process of applying knowledge to make work easier.

In these books, children are encouraged to explore the early inspirations for machines, and the process of modification that has brought them forward in their current state, and in doing so, come to an understanding of the design process.

The simple text and humorous illustrations give a clear explanation of how these machines actually work, and experiments and activities give suggestions for further practical exploration.

Suggestions for further activities

*   Visit a building site and look at how pulleys are used, i.e. to lift building materials up scaffolding using cranes, etc.

*   Experiment using different weights with a real pulley wheel. Can you add extra pulley wheels to enable you to lift heavier weights?

*   Make a display of pictures from magazines or catalogues of different machines or pulleys.

Further information

Amazing Science: Forces and Motion by Sally Hewitt (Wayland, 2007)

Simple Machines: Pulleys by Chris Oxlade (Franklin Watts, 2007)

Little Bees: Push it, Pull it by Claire Llewellyn (Wayland, 2009)

Ways into Science: Push and Pull by Peter Riley (Franklin Watts, 2007)

Adult Reference

The Way Things Work by David Macaulay and Neil Ardley (Dorling Kindersley, 2004)

Available as DVD (Dorling Kindersley, 2005)

Index